Letters for Tomorrow

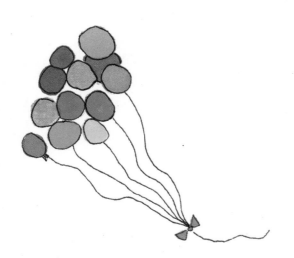

A Journal for Expectant Moms and Dads

MAIN
STREET
BOOKS

DOUBLEDAY

NEW YORK   LONDON   TORONTO   SYDNEY   AUCKLAND

Letters for Tomorrow

ROBIN FREEMAN
BERNSTEIN, M.A.
AND
CATHY MOORE,
PH.D.

ILLUSTRATIONS
BY
LISA FREEMAN

A Main Street Book

PUBLISHED BY DOUBLEDAY

a division of Bantam Doubleday Dell Publishing Group, Inc.

1540 Broadway, New York, New York 10036

MAIN STREET BOOKS, DOUBLEDAY, and the portrayal of a building with a tree are trademarks of Doubleday, a division of Bantam Doubleday Dell Publishing Group, Inc.

Book Design by Gretchen Achilles
Calligraphy by Dorothy Urlich

Library of Congress Cataloging-in-Publication Data

Bernstein, Robin Freeman, 1954–
    Letters for tomorrow / written by Robin Freeman Bernstein and Cathy Moore.
      p.   cm.
    "A Main Street book."
    I. Pregnancy—Popular works.   2. Parent and infant.   I. Moore, Cathy,
1951–   . II. Title.
RG525.B47   1995
618.2′4—dc20   94-9466
                                  CIP

ISBN 0-385-47515-2

Copyright © 1995 by Robin Freeman Bernstein and Cathy Moore

All Rights Reserved

Printed in Italy
February 1995
First Edition

1   3   5   7   9   10   8   6   4   2

Contents

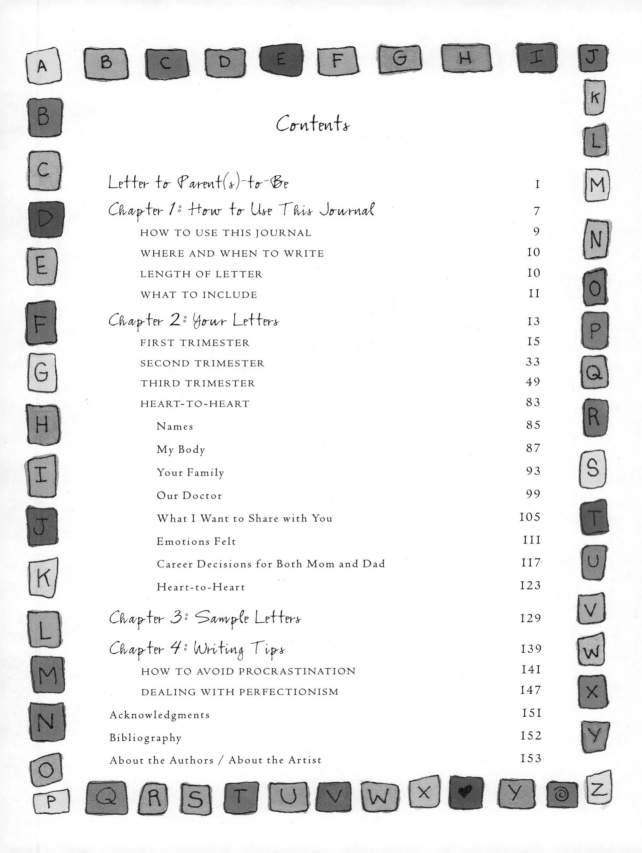

Letter to Parent (s)-to-Be

What cannot letters inspire? They have souls; they can speak; they have in them all that force which expresses the transports of the heart; they have all the fire of our passions.

—*Letter from Héloïse to Abelard*

Dear Parent(s)-to-Be:

It is with great enthusiasm and delight that we begin this letter to you. First, let us congratulate you on your pregnancy. What an exciting, overwhelming, and miraculous time you have entered into. As mothers, we too remember the emotional and physical feelings of our own pregnancies—being in shock, awe, and amazement, wondering why they called it "morning sickness" when it lasted twenty-four hours a day, watching our bodies change, feeling the baby kick. We also remember our partners during pregnancy: their visits with us to the doctor; having them gain weight right along with us; attending Lamaze classes together; and watching them oftentimes feel helpless, wishing they could carry more of the responsibility. Individually and together, we realized our lives as we once knew them would be totally new and different from now on.

So it is in your and your baby's honor that we have created *Letters for Tomorrow: A Journal for Expectant Moms and Dads*. In your hands you have a guide to help you write a collection of letters to your child documenting your pregnancy. You will see as you read on that the journal is in an easy-to-follow, outlined format through which you can express your thoughts, feelings, and experiences to your child. Once you start your letter, if by chance you find you're having difficulty with where to find inspiration or with procrastination or with deciding what you want to write about, the ideas included in this book will help you. Through the writing of these letters you will begin to develop honest, open, loving communication with your soon-to-be-born child, thus creating a strong bond with your child prior to birth. As mothers and therapists we believe communication is the backbone of all healthy and loving relationships.

During the nine months of pregnancy, there are so many special moments to remember. This journal is the perfect way to hold on to them forever. This period is the only time in your child's life when there won't be a camera or video recorder available to document his or her growth. The art of letter writing allows you to create a lifelong treasure to be passed from parent to child. Expectant parents have told us over and over how valuable the writing of these letters was for them personally: how they immediately bonded with their child the moment he or she was placed in their arms, how easy it was to talk with the infant and share their feelings. They also told us how the communication with their partner was enhanced when writing letters together.

Letters for Tomorrow provides you, the parent-to-be, with a head start. It's drawn from our experience as both licensed mental health professionals and mothers. Included are ideas on how to use the journal; suggested topics upon which you may choose to base your letters; beautifully designed journal pages; inspirational thoughts; places to paste in photographs; sample letters from other parents-to-be; and even pages for expectant grandparents, siblings, pets, godparents, and other family members and friends to write their letters on; writing tips. The journal travels with you through the many exciting experiences of pregnancy—we've offered suggested letter topics in chronological order by trimester, from "Today I found out I'm pregnant" through "Time for your birth." You can use the journal like a diary to document event-by-event what is happening. And you can also use it as a calendar to flip ahead and catch a glimpse of the near future—to anticipate as well as prepare for events in your pregnancy such as touring the hospital, making career decisions, beginning childbirth class, enjoying your baby shower, and meeting the baby's pediatrician. We feel the design of the journal will open your creativity and give you an extra boost of confidence to freely express yourself, removing any roadblocks to allow the writer within to emerge.

In closing, we'd like to share a special passage from the book *Gift of a Letter* by Alexandra Stoddard.

Letters are magical . . . They open doors to innumerable emotions and experiences. Letters document the chapters in our lives—our discoveries, our passions, our sorrows and growth as well as all the ebb and flow inevitable in life. Letters allow us to be personal, natural and specific. More than any other medium, letters provide an uninhibited view of everyday life—the most accurate and natural form of autobiography . . . They are detailed; they act as a zoom lens into specific moments, experiences and emotions . . . Scenes are painted, stories are told that linger as long as the letter, and beyond.

Once again, our congratulations to you and the newest member of your family. May the writing of these letters provide you and your little one with clarity, understanding, peace, and love.

With much admiration and respect,
Robin and Cathy

Chapter 1

How to Use This Journal

. . . only on paper has humanity achieved glory, beauty, truth, knowledge, virtue and abiding love.

—*George Bernard Shaw*

How to Use This Journal

The format we have created for your journal is very easy to follow, including pages with suggested letter topics for each trimester. We have highlighted the exciting and memorable experiences we all share, also leaving room for you to write letters about experiences unique to your new family. Feel free to use the journal as a diary or as a calendar—to write about what's going on currently or to catch a glimpse of what's ahead in your future.

Please remember there is no set way to use the journal. If the topics we suggest don't inspire you, feel free to write letters of your own choice on the blank pages instead. However, if you need guidance there are essentially two points to remember:

a. After reading Chapter 1, turn to Chapter 2, "Your Letters," where you will find four sections: "First Trimester," "Second Trimester," "Third Trimester," and "Heart-to-Heart." The first three sections contain topics specific to each trimester. The last section suggests topics that can be written about anytime throughout the pregnancy. An important note: *It is okay to start the journal at any point in your pregnancy.* Locate the section in "Your Letters" that is right for you and begin.

b. You will notice in Chapter 2 that the first three sections provide a topic for you to write about on each individual journal page. Also included in these sections are blank journal pages for you to write about a topic of your choice. The final section, "Heart-to-Heart," includes topics that may arise throughout your pregnancy. Some of these may apply to you and some of them may not. Therefore, instead of devoting a whole journal page to each of these topics. we've listed them together under headings such as "Your Family," "Our Doctor," and "What I Want to Share with You." If a topic in one of these areas inspires you, just flip to one of the blank pages and write your letter. On all the journal pages space is provided for you to record the date, who the letter is from, and the age of your soon-to-be-born child. Have fun!

Where and When to Write

Take a moment and ask yourself, "When I write, what works best for me? Under what conditions do I do my best writing?"

Some people are able to keep up with a journal anywhere—in a subway, train, airplane, or restaurant. Others need a quiet environment.

Sometimes the place itself where you choose to write can inspire a letter, such as:

Dear Baby,

We are flying high above California on our way to New York. This is the last business trip we will be taking. Dr. Weinberger says it's time for us to stay on the ground. So . . . we'll be doing a lot of nesting together. Oh boy, we're having a little turbulence, or is that you kicking? Just kidding. Time to go. 'Bye.

Love,

Mommy

Length of Letter

The letters you write can be short (one or two sentences) or long (many pages). There is no set length for your letters. It's amazing how sometimes a few words can paint such a special memory.

Dear Grandchild,

  I went to the cemetery this morning to bring your grandma her weekly flowers. I told her all about you. I know she heard me.

  Love,

  Grandpa

What to Include

When we conducted our research for the journal, many parents-to-be asked us, "What should I include in my letters?" Anything you want! However, we have found that what does help you to paint an enduring and vivid picture is to keep the following in mind while you are writing:

1. Your experiences and thoughts that day, week, morning, month . . .

2. How you are feeling:

   - Happy
   - Anxious
   - Excited
   - Nervous
   - Overwhelmed
   - Uncomfortable
   - Scared
   - Fantastic
   - Loving
   - Hungry
   - Emotional
   - Sensitive

3. The time of day

4. The weather

5. Your location while writing

6. Who is with you while you're writing your letter

Chapter 2

Your Letters

Sit by a crackling fire and read some of your favorite letters. While sitting there soaking up all the love and support, think of one person you love and write a beautiful, loving letter to that person. Let the flame in your hearth warm your heart. One letter in a lifetime to a mother, a daughter or a special friend could make a greater difference than you dare to believe.

—*Alexandra Stoddard*
GIFT OF A LETTER

First Trimester

Date:

From:

Baby's Age:

Topic: Today I (we) found out
I'm (we're) pregnant . . .

Date:

From:

Baby's Age:

Topic: The first person I (we)
told was . . .

_____
_____
_____
_____
_____
_____
_____
_____
_____
_____
_____
_____
_____
_____
_____
_____
_____
_____
_____
_____
_____
_____
_____
_____

Date:

From:

Baby's Age:

Topic: Here's a picture of me
      newly pregnant . . .

Date:

From:

Baby's Age:

Topic: Here's a picture of your
parents . . .

Date:

From:

Baby's Age:

Topic: I've (we've) waited for
so long . . .

Date:

From:

Baby's Age:

Topic: My (our) feelings about
being pregnant . . .

_____
_____
_____
_____
_____
_____
_____
_____
_____
_____
_____
_____
_____
_____
_____
_____
_____
_____
_____
_____
_____
_____
_____

Date:

From:

Baby's Age:

Topic: Our first doctor's visit . . .

Date:

From:

Baby's Age:

Topic: I (we) heard your heartbeat
for the first time . . .

Date:

From:

Baby's Age:

Topic: Here's a picture of us at
two months . . .

Date:

From:

Baby's Age:

Topic: I find myself driving extra
carefully . . .

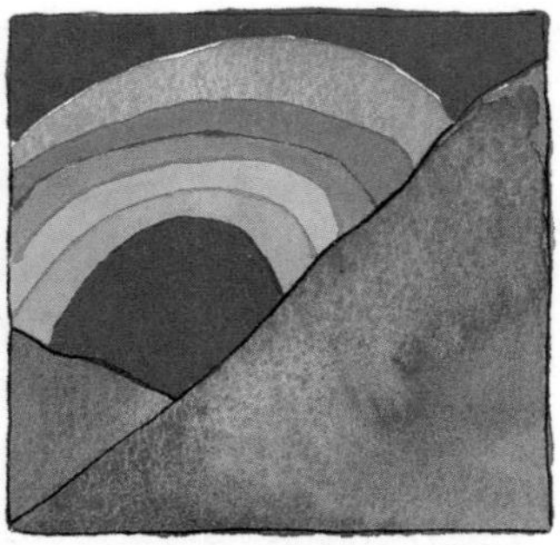

_____

_____

_____

_____

_____

_____

_____

_____

_____

_____

_____

_____

_____

_____

_____

_____

_____

_____

_____

_____

_____

_____

_____

_____

_____

Date:

From:

Baby's Age:

Topic: Body changes I'm
       experiencing . . .

Date:

From:

Baby's Age:

Topic: Here's a picture of us at
three months . . .

Date:

From:

Baby's Age:

Topic: Notes to my (our) child . . .

Date:

From:

Baby's Age:

Topic: Notes to my (our) child . . .

Date:

From:

Baby's Age:

Topic: Notes to my (our) child . . .

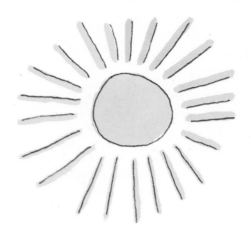

Second Trimester

Date:

From:

Baby's Age:

Topic: We're entering the second
trimester. Here we are . . .

Date:

From:

Baby's Age:

Topic: You had your first picture
taken. It's called an
ultrasound . . .

_____

_____

_____

_____

_____

_____

Date:

From:

Baby's Age:

Topic: I had an amniocentesis . . .

Date:

From:

Baby's Age:

Topic: I (we) found out you're a
boy/girl . . .

Date:

From:

Baby's Age:

Topic: Here's a picture of us at four months . . .

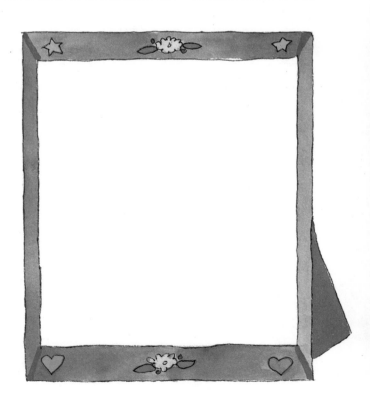

Date:

From:

Baby's Age:

Topic: I (we) felt you move/kick
for the first time . . .

Date:

From:

Baby's Age:

Topic: You're moving around more
and more . . .

Date:

From:

Baby's Age:

Topic: Today people commented on how much I've grown with you . . .

Date:

From:

Baby's Age:

Topic: Here's a picture of us at five months . . .

Date:

From:

Baby's Age:

Topic: I (we) started shopping for
your furniture today...

Date:

From:

Baby's Age:

Topic: Body changes I'm experiencing . . .

_____
_____
_____
_____
_____
_____
_____
_____
_____
_____
_____
_____
_____
_____
_____
_____
_____
_____
_____
_____
_____
_____
_____
_____
_____

Date:

From:

Baby's Age:

Topic: Here's a picture of us at six
months . . .

_____

_____

_____

_____

_____

_____

_____

Date:

From:

Baby's Age:

Topic: Notes to my (our) child . . .

Date:

From:

Baby's Age:

Topic: Notes to my (our) child . . .

_____

_____

_____

_____

_____

_____

_____

_____

_____

_____

_____

_____

_____

_____

_____

_____

_____

_____

_____

_____

_____

_____

_____

_____

_____

_____

Third Trimester

Date:

From:

Baby's Age:

Topic: We're entering the third
trimester. Here we are . . .

Date:

From:

Baby's Age:

Topic: You're moving around more
and more . . .

Date:

From:

Baby's Age:

Topic: Your sleeping patterns . . .

_____

_____

_____

_____

_____

_____

_____

_____

_____

_____

_____

_____

_____

_____

_____

_____

_____

_____

_____

_____

_____

_____

Date:

From:

Baby's Age:

Topic: Here's a picture of us at seven months . . .

Date:

From:

Baby's Age:

Topic: I'm wondering if I'll know
when I'm in labor . . .

_____

_____

_____

_____

_____

_____

_____

_____

_____

_____

_____

_____

_____

_____

_____

_____

_____

_____

_____

_____

_____

_____

_____

_____

Date:

From:

Baby's Age:

Topic: We took a tour of the
hospital . . .

Date:

From:

Baby's Age:

Topic: I'm (we're) ready to start childbirth classes . . .

Date:

From:

Baby's Age:

Topic: The first childbirth
class . . .

Date:

From:

Baby's Age:

Topic: I (we) can't believe it's only
_____ (how long) and you'll
be in my (our) arms . . .

Date:

From:

Baby's Age:

Topic: I've (we've) decided how to
        decorate your room . . .

_____

_____

_____

_____

_____

_____

_____

_____

_____

_____

_____

_____

_____

_____

_____

_____

_____

_____

_____

_____

Date:

From:

Baby's Age:

Topic: I (we) chose your bedroom furniture...

Date:

From:

Baby's Age:

Topic: Your crib was set up . . .

Date:

From:

Baby's Age:

Topic: Here's a picture of your
room . . .

_____
_____
_____
_____
_____
_____
_____
_____
_____
_____

_____
_____
_____
_____
_____
_____

Date:

From:

Baby's Age:

Topic: There was a baby shower
for you . . .

Date:

From:

Baby's Age:

Topic: Here are pictures from
        our shower . . .

Date:

From:

Baby's Age:

Topic: I'd (we'd) like you to meet some of your family. Here are their pictures . . .

Date:

From:

Baby's Age:

Topic: I'm starting to feel more
energetic now . . .

Date:

From:

Baby's Age:

Topic: I (we) met your
pediatrician today . . .

Date:

From:

Baby's Age:

Topic: My health throughout the
pregnancy has been . . .

Date:

From:

Baby's Age:

Topic: I'm nesting . . .

Date:

From:

Baby's Age:

Topic: I'm nesting . . .

Date:

From:

Baby's Age:

Topic: Body changes I'm
experiencing . . .

Date:

From:

Baby's Age:

Topic: I've (we've) packed the bag
for the hospital . . .

_____

_____

_____

_____

_____

_____

_____

_____

_____

_____

_____

_____

_____

_____

_____

_____

_____

_____

_____

_____

_____

_____

_____

_____

Date:

From:

Baby's Age:

Topic: I'm (we're) so ready for you to be born . . .

Date:

From:

Baby's Age:

Topic: I (we) can't wait to meet
you face-to-face . . .

_____

_____

_____

_____

_____

_____

_____

_____

_____

_____

_____

_____

_____

_____

_____

_____

_____

_____

_____

_____

_____

_____

_____

Date:

From:

Baby's Age:

Topic: Here's a picture of us at
nine months . . .

Date:

From:

Baby's Age:

Topic: We're in labor ... now ...

Date:

From:

Baby's Age:

Topic: Here we are in the
hospital . . .

Date:

From:

Baby's Age:

Topic: Time for your birth . . .

Date:

From:

Baby's Age:

Topic: You are born!

Date:

From:

Baby's Age:

Topic: These photos were taken
right after you were born . . .

Date:

From:

Baby's Age:

Topic: Notes to my (our) child . . .

Date:

From:

Baby's Age:

Topic: Notes to my (our) child . . .

Heart-to-Heart

Names

Possible names if you're a girl . . .

_____

_____

_____

_____

Possible names if you're a boy . . .

_____

_____

_____

_____

We're thinking of naming you after . . .

_____

_____

_____

_____

My Body

- Body changes I'm experiencing while pregnant . . .

- My (our) food cravings are . . .

- My (our) food aversions are . . .

- My friend the bathroom . . .

- Do I love naps . . .

- Do I wish I had time to take naps . . .

- Call me forgetful, I'm so absentminded . . .

- My exercise program since pregnancy . . .

Date:

From:

Baby's Age:

Topic:

Date:

From:

Baby's Age:

Topic:

Date:

From:

Baby's Age:

Topic:

Date:

From:

Baby's Age:

Topic:

Your Family

- Dad's autobiography . . .

- Our dating history . . .

- You have a brother(s)/sister(s)/pet(s) waiting to meet you . . .

- There's someone special I want you to know . . .

- Letters from family members . . .

- Mom's autobiography . . .

Date:

From:

Baby's Age:

Topic:

Date:

From:

Baby's Age:

Topic:

Date:

From:

Baby's Age:

Topic:

Date:

From:

Baby's Age:

Topic:

Date:

From:

Baby's Age:

Topic:

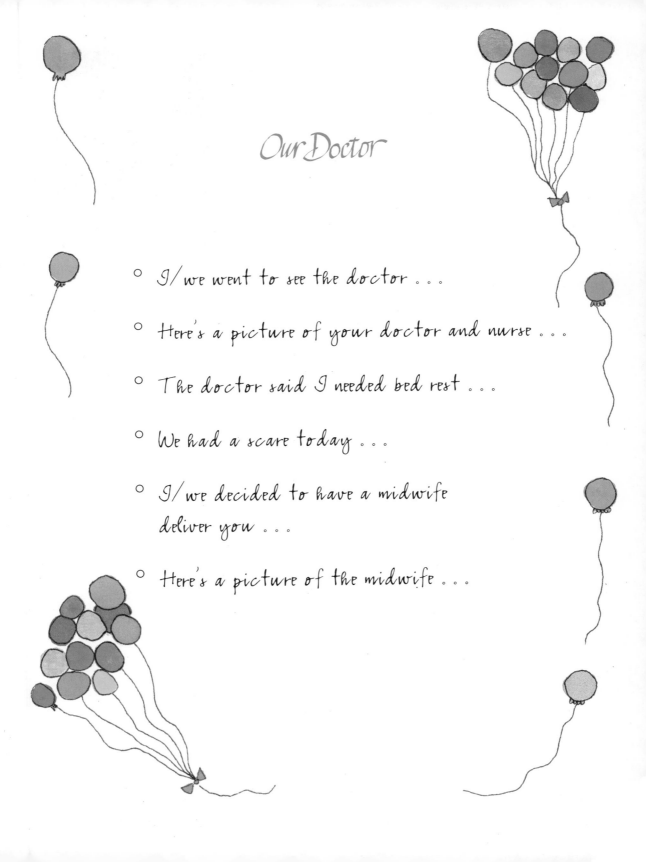

Our Doctor

- ○ I/we went to see the doctor . . .

- ○ Here's a picture of your doctor and nurse . . .

- ○ The doctor said I needed bed rest . . .

- ○ We had a scare today . . .

- ○ I/we decided to have a midwife deliver you . . .

- ○ Here's a picture of the midwife . . .

Date:

From:

Baby's Age:

Topic:

_____
_____
_____
_____
_____
_____
_____
_____
_____
_____
_____
_____
_____
_____
_____
_____
_____
_____
_____
_____
_____
_____
_____
_____

Date:

From:

Baby's Age:

Topic:

_____

_____

_____

_____

_____

_____

_____

_____

_____

_____

_____

_____

_____

_____

_____

_____

_____

_____

_____

_____

_____

_____

_____

_____

_____

_____

_____

_____

Date:

From:

Baby's Age:

Topic:

_____

_____

_____

_____

_____

_____

_____

_____

_____

_____

_____

_____

_____

_____

_____

_____

_____

_____

_____

_____

_____

_____

_____

_____

_____

Date:

From:

Baby's Age:

Topic:

What I Want to Share with You

- Songs and Music

- Books

- Words of Wisdom

- Friends

- Sports

- Nature

Date:

From:

Baby's Age:

Topic:

Date:

From:

Baby's Age:

Topic:

Date:

From:

Baby's Age:

Topic:

Date:

From:

Baby's Age:

Topic:

Emotions Felt

- Fear . . .

- Excitement . . .

- Hope . . .

- Misgiving . . .

- Joy . . .

- Worry . . .

- Happiness . . .

- Bliss . . .

- Exhaustion . . .

Date:

From:

Baby's Age:

Topic:

Date:

From:

Baby's Age:

Topic:

Date:

From:

Baby's Age:

Topic:

Date:

From:

Baby's Age:

Topic:

Career Decisions for Both
Mom and Dad

- I'm scared I won't want to go back to work once you're born, yet I know I have to . . .

- I wish I could stay home with you . . .

- I've worked so hard at my career. I'm torn . . .

- I'm going to work part-time when you're born . . .

- My mom was a working mom, and because of my experience as a child I've decided . . .

- My mom was a stay-at-home mom, and because of my experience as a child I've decided . . .

- The decision I've made about my career might change over time as we grow . . .

Date:

From:

Baby's Age:

Topic:

Date:

From:

Baby's Age:

Topic:

Date:

From:

Baby's Age:

Topic:

_____

_____

_____

_____

_____

_____

_____

_____

_____

_____

_____

_____

_____

_____

_____

_____

_____

_____

_____

_____

_____

_____

_____

Date:

From:

Baby's Age:

Topic:

_____

_____

_____

_____

_____

_____

_____

_____

_____

_____

_____

_____

_____

_____

_____

_____

_____

_____

_____

_____

_____

_____

_____

_____

Date:

From:

Baby's Age:

Topic:

Heart-to-Heart

○ You are a miracle . . .

○ Last night I dreamed . . .

○ I (we) hope you're healthy and fine . . .

○ My (our) prayer for you is . . .

○ Life is tough right now . . .

○ There's a special person I (we) want
you to know . . .

○ My daydreams of you are . . .

Date:
From:
Baby's Age:
Topic:

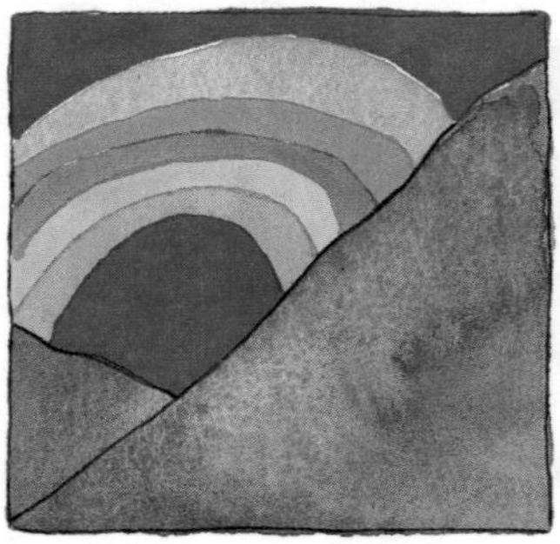

Date:

From:

Baby's Age:

Topic:

Date:

From:

Baby's Age:

Topic:

Date:

From:

Baby's Age:

Topic:

Chapter 3

Sample Letters

What lies behind us and what lies before us are tiny matters compared to what lies within us.

—*Ralph Waldo Emerson*

Date: July 6, 1988
From: Mom
Baby's Age: Sixteen weeks in utero
Topic: I felt you move for the first time . . .

Hello, Little One,

Your dad is at work tonight, so I have some quiet time to sit down and catch you up on all the truly wonderful things we've been experiencing together.

One afternoon I was sitting in the shade relaxing, with my hands rubbing my round belly sending you much love, when the most amazing thing happened. I felt you kick and I felt you moving around. At first I didn't know what to do. I looked over at your dad, who was engrossed in a book. Then I looked over at our friends Mitchel and Dayna; they were sleeping. Suddenly I felt you move again. I called out to your dad to come over. He could hear the urgency in my voice and came to my side. I took his hand and placed it on my belly, and told him I'd felt you move. We stared into each other's eyes and waited. Then you kicked nice and strong. Tears of joy, awe, and wonder were in our eyes. It had to be one of the most exciting moments of our lives. Dayna quickly came over and said she wanted to be a part of this, too. She placed her hand on the magic spot and . . . she felt you also.

What a miracle you are. Since that special moment, I have felt you begin to move more and more often . . . and it still takes my breath away. I'm sure in life we will have our ups and downs as a family, and yet there is one thing your dad and I want you to know and remember . . . we love you with all our hearts.

Rest well, little one,

With much love,
Mom (and Dad in spirit)

Date: April 17, 1991
From: Mom and Dad
Baby's Age: Twenty-four weeks in utero
Topic: We had a scare today . . .

Dear Baby,

Tonight I had a little scare. I was teaching at Gymboree, and my classes were over. I went to the bathroom, and there was a little blood on the toilet paper. I thought you were coming early. I talked to you the whole time I was closing up the site, telling you that whatever happened, it would be all right, that we'd get ahold of Daddy, and that you were going to be fine. Inside I was panicked. Your room isn't ready, I don't know if you are "ready." I was scared. Daddy and I agreed that we should get a beeper, and I should have the phone number at his acting class, just in case. We're going to call the doctor tomorrow to make sure everything is okay. You're moving inside me right now, and that reassures me. Take your time, honey, and make sure that you're ready, and we'll make sure your room is ready for you. We love you.

Mom and Dad

Date: October 3, 1990
From: Mom and Dad
Baby's Age: One week in utero
Topic: Today I found out we're pregnant . . .

Dear Baby,

Today we found out you were on your way. We have only been trying for a month to get pregnant, so the news was a bit surprising.

I'm thirty-two years old and Dad just turned thirty-eight this past August, although we tell everyone in show business that he's only thirty-four. We're both actors, but right now we're both waiters. I've started school at UCLA to become a personal trainer, so I won't ever have to waiter again.

Anyway, given our present financial situation, we're a little apprehensive about how soon you'll be here. I think we thought it would take longer to get pregnant. I want so much for you, and it would be great if you were never without; but whatever our situation, you couldn't be more loved, and you're only probably a week or so old.

Your dad and I love each other very, very much and are looking forward to bringing a life made with that love into the world.

Well, it's late, and I have a big audition tomorrow. Good night, Little One, we love you.

Mom and Dad

P.S. You have a great dog named Emmett, too!

Date: August 20, 1988
From: Dad
Baby's Age: Approximately twenty-eight weeks in utero
Topic: Today we learned you are a boy . . .

Our Beautiful Child,

Well, it has been too long since our last letter, but so much has happened that I thought we'd better write tonight. It's after midnight and I have just enough energy to tell you some very important things.

First and foremost . . . we found out two weeks ago at our last ultrasound that you are a growing and healthy little boy! That's right, we saw it for ourselves right there in black and white. I asked Dr. Francis if it was possible that we might be fooled by the picture—that maybe what looked like a penis might just be an umbilical cord. He said there was no mistake. You were very active inside your mother that day; your arms and legs were in constant motion. And we both were so excited we were going to have a little boy . . . You will be the one to carry on the Bernstein name when you get old enough to understand what that means. Your mom and I have been excitedly trying to set up your room now that we know a little about you.

Excuse me, my son, but I realize I'm rambling a bit. I must be more tired than I care to admit right now. I want to continue, though, for a while more. My son . . . those words are still so new and so miraculous for me (and your beautiful mom) to say. To think that soon we will give birth to a handsome baby boy is such a wonderful thing to look forward to . . . The entire family is patiently awaiting your arrival around December 15. Being the first boy in these families since me is considered a real event.

For now, I say good night, sleep tight! We love you . . .

Your dad

Date: October 9, 1990
From: Dad
Baby's Age: Two weeks in utero
Topic: Feelings and thoughts about being a new Dad . . .

Can you hold on a second while I talk to our friend Otto in New York? I thought so. I'm back, your mother is talking to him now. So, how was your day? Mine was mostly about you and your mother. I cleaned house, and shopped and cooked to feed the two of you, and the most interesting thing happened. While I was driving home from the Co-Op with cousin Ed, I was struck with the thought of how exclusive the birth process is, that relationship (for lack of a better word) that the two of you share. I mean you are so very young right now, and growing inside her. Growing inside my wife. Your mother has so much responsibility placed on her, every day, and I can't ever really touch that, or experience it in the same way. This is not bitterness, mind you, more a sense of envy and curiosity. What you must feel like. Amazing. I love you both.

Sleep well,
Dad

Date: November 10, 1990
From: Mom and Dad
Baby's Age: Seven weeks in utero
Topic: There's a special person we want you to know . . .

Dear Baby,

After a week of great strength, Grandpa Bo died early this morning. His nurse told us how quick and peaceful it was, and that he spoke of seeing birds sometimes before his death. Obviously angels came to mind, and fed our thoughts with wonder and hope—what if? It seems that after the magic of you anything is possible. We do so want to believe that he is in a much better place, starting a better journey. Godspeed to you and Grandpa Bo.

We love you both,
Dad and Mom

Date: November 23, 1990
From: Mom and Dad
Baby's Age: Nine and a half weeks in utero
Topic: Life is tough right now . . .

Dear Baby,

I don't feel much like talking tonight. I think both your dad and I are really growing tired of the struggle. Daddy's still fighting the blues, and I'm tired all the time. Sometimes I feel as if everything that's occurred within the last two months has just caught up to me and I can't take one more step. Everything seems overwhelming, and I just want to escape for two or three weeks and just lie around in beautiful surroundings. Please God, let there be a break in the weather of our lives. Let the sun shine and the flowers bloom and our energies be restored. We're trying so hard, Baby.

We love you,
Mom and Dad

Date: May 28, 1991—12:10 A.M.
From: Dad and Mom
Baby's Age: Thirty-five weeks
Topic: Time for your birth . . .

Hi Sweetheart,

It's Daddy here; just a last quick note of love and encouragement. This is going to be quite a day for all of us, and just like this world, it is going to be tough, but wonderful and worth it all. We love you so, and we love each other so; what a beautiful way to start a family. See you later this morning.

Love,
Dad and Mom

Date: October 10, 1991

From: Brother

Baby's Age: Thirty-three weeks

Topic: Sibling letter about baby's arrival

Dear Baby,

My mom and dad told me I'm going to have a little brother. You can stay a few days and then we'll take you back to the hospital.

Love,
Ethan
Age five

Chapter 4

Writing Tips

Words are the voice of the heart.

—*Confucius*

How to Avoid Procrastination

Procrastination: *The habit of postponing until tomorrow what could be done today.*

If you have the tendency to put things off until the last possible moment and don't understand why you do this, the following section is especially for you.

Parents-to-be put off writing their letters for specific reasons. In our work with journal writers we have found that the most common reasons they procrastinate writing are because they keep themselves very busy; they are waiting for the perfect moment and mood to write; they feel overwhelmed; or, most important and more serious, they feel inadequate in their ability to express their thoughts, emotions, and experiences.

You may possibly see in yourself some or all of these reasons for putting off the writing of your letters. We encourage you to read on as we provide you with guidelines to assist you in avoiding procrastination.

PRODUCTIVE AVOIDANCE, OR EXCESSIVE BUSYNESS

Productive avoidance is when you find yourself doing everything possible to avoid the real task at hand—writing.

Screenwriters and other professional writers tell us they'll often sit down at their computers to write, when suddenly an assortment of tasks come to mind—productive tasks, such as watering plants and paying bills. Before they know it, they are engrossed in these distractions, totally avoiding what they set out to accomplish.

In reference to people who procrastinate through productive avoidance, John Sabini, Ph.D., professor of psychology at the University of Pennsylvania, says, "They can't face the loss of their self-esteem of admitting they are not going to work on their project, so they find themselves frittering away a lot of time on other things they never would have done otherwise."

Common forms of productive avoidance are returning phone calls, walking the dog, cleaning, or getting organized.

The following are a few ways you can effectively work on this issue:

a. A technique or tool we use with our clients is to have them make a list of their various forms of productive avoidance. We suggest that you take a moment and make a list for yourself. If your list is sparse, you may have to wait until you are ready to write a letter, when this form of procrastination is at its peak. (This can be a great time to complete your list.) Once you uncover behaviors that prevent you from writing, you can take charge of them. Your list is the beginning of that process. It will become easier and easier to recognize when you are productively delaying writing.

My forms of productive avoidance:

1.

2.

3.

4.

5.

b. Once you have recognized that you are productively avoiding writing, STOP whatever you are doing and go straight to the task you are putting off—in this case writing a letter in this journal. Choose a topic and begin writing for a specific time (try five minutes).

c. If you are still having difficulty writing, turn to a page in your journal and write a letter on the following topic:

Dear Little One,
Right now I'm having trouble choosing a topic and writing . . .

This is a wonderful opportunity to begin a process of honest self-disclosure, which is a very valuable form of communication. Here you can show your child that you are human and that when you have a problem, you can openly communicate about it.

WAITING FOR THE RIGHT MOMENT TO WRITE

Let's look at the statements and excuses often used in this form of procrastination:

1. "I'll write when I have more energy."
2. "When my husband/wife/partner gets home we'll write together."
3. "On the weekend I'll be in the mood."
4. "I want to return these phone calls first."
5. "I might be interrupted."

"Procrastinators tend to wait for the perfect conditions to deal with their problem rather than setting a brief time during the day to address it," says Dr. Robert Boice, Ph.D., professor of psychology and director of the Faculty Instructional Support Office at the State University of New York at Stony Brook, in his book *Do It Now*.

There is no perfect moment to write. This is a myth. Many of the exciting and wonderful moments will slip right by if you get caught in this trap.

FEELING OVERWHELMED

Just being pregnant can be overwhelming to parents-to-be. You might experience this for any of the following reasons:

1. Being responsible for a new baby

2. Financial concerns

3. Living arrangements

4. Child care

5. Health concerns of the mother-to-be

These are just a sample of the feelings you might experience throughout your pregnancy. When you do (and you will), we suggest writing in your journal to help cope with them.

If you find you are feeling overwhelmed:

Choose a topic and write a sentence, an update rather than a letter. You can always go back and fill in the details later if you wish.

We have used this form of problem solving with our clients for many years now. Two particular cases come to mind. One was a woman who encountered a scare in her sixth month of pregnancy. She went into premature labor. The doctors were able to stop the labor and the baby was born full-term. However, after the scare, the woman noticed that she didn't want to write letters anymore. When we looked into this further, we discovered that she felt very close to her child when she wrote and she was afraid to risk that feeling of closeness. She was so terrified of feeling any closer to her child until it was born that she stopped writing altogether.

In the other case, a woman had received a major job promotion toward the end of her pregnancy. She had been working for this promotion for many years. It involved weekly travel, being away from home two days and nights per week. The client was overwhelmed and in tremendous conflict and also stopped writing. Starting with one sentence helped her overcome these feelings.

Most people, when they feel emotionally overwhelmed, go into a shell (confronting the issue usually means emotional pain—tears, anxiety, fears, anger—or at least discomfort). They just hope that things will take care of themselves. However, as time passes, things don't take care of themselves, and they only become more anxious. Some of our clients in this situation were provided with a few topics to write about:

Dear Little One, I am feeling overwhelmed . . .
Dear Little One, I am scared to write about . . .
Dear Little One, What I'm scared to face is . . .

At first they were only able to write the topic. As they persevered, they were able to write a sentence or two; finally they were able to write letters about what was going on within themselves. When their children were born, they had worked through their issues and felt resolution about some of their problems, and the closeness they were once scared to feel was very strong and no longer scary. Bonding had taken place in utero.

If you are experiencing these feelings, we encourage you to go forward rather than retreat. The results can only be positive and rewarding.

FEAR AND DOUBT ABOUT HOW TO COMMUNICATE

We feel that this is the most important reason for procrastination. This type of procrastination is the tendency to put off communicating or to hold inside one's feelings, thoughts, wishes, or needs. People who do this have most likely never learned how to communicate. It has been our experience that people who were not taught and did not learn how to express themselves can be reluctant to begin and be consistent with the letter-writing process. We'd like to give you some information to help you build your confidence about becoming a clear and strong communicator.

The following case history might help you understand this issue more clearly. We had the opportunity to work with a couple in a seminar we gave for parents-to-be on journal writing. Both partners had been taught by their parents that one's feelings were meant to be kept to oneself, that children were to be seen and not heard. So for many years they each held all their emotions inside, feeling tremendously guilty whenever they let them out (or whenever they talked about them). The couple attended the seminar because they were procrastinating about writing their letters and wanted to make sure they didn't pass on the message that feelings are to be kept inside to their child.

We spoke with them about two very valuable communication skills—"self-disclosure" and "I-statements"—and how these could help them to stop procrastinating.

"Self-disclosure" is when a person talks openly and honestly with another about his or her feelings, thoughts, wishes, or needs. When one does this with another it produces close, warm, and intimate feelings between the people involved. The first step is taking the risk to state a feeling to another person. With the couple we just discussed, we taught them to first ask themselves, what do I feel right now? We taught them to write down or list *all* of the feelings at that moment.

Next, we taught them to state their feelings to each other by using the second technique, I-statements. The following phrases are some beginnings of I-statements that demonstrate healthy communication. You are welcome to use them in the writing of your letters.

I am feeling (happy, anxious, confused, angry, excited, etc.)
I want you to know . . .
I wish for you/me/us . . .
Today I experienced . . .
I need . . .
I want . . .

As you can see, all of the above examples include the word "I." I-statements are the key to effective communication. When a person begins a message with an I-statement the receiver is receptive and able to hear what is being said. On the other hand, when a person communicates by using "you-statements" (e.g., "It's your fault," "Why didn't you?" "You made me feel . . ." "If it wasn't for you I'd be able to . . .") the receiver automatically stops listening, shuts down inside, and starts defending himself or herself. When this happens the process of communication stops. In writing your letters we encourage you to practice using I-statements, thus reinforcing a new habit of healthy communication.

Through these exercises, the couple began to feel safe communicating their feelings and thoughts with each other. They could then share this new-found closeness in their letters to their child-to-be. Because of their willingness to take the risk to begin to reveal themselves to one another and their soon-to-be-born child, they were able to stop the pattern of communication that had been passed on to them and begin a fresh and new one with their own child.

Many newborn parents have expressed sheer delight in the closeness they felt with their child when he or she was born. They remark over and over how the writing process gave them the opportunity to overcome procrastination and take charge of communicating their feelings and thoughts.

You have in your hands a powerful tool to begin a lifelong process—the process of communication. Start visiting and talking with your child-to-be. Begin to create that special bond that only a parent and child share. You will watch a closeness develop that will be invaluable and irreplaceable. You will also be sharing your true self with your child.

Dealing with Perfectionism

As therapists, we have worked with clients who hope to write the "perfect" letter or journal entry. There are three types of perfectionists when it comes to letter/journal writing. The first type tries desperately to avoid crossed-out words, different-colored inks, misspelled words, ink or food smudges, run-on sentences, incorrect grammar, etc. What ends up happening with this type of perfectionist is that letters are constantly rewritten, pages are torn out, journal entries are not completed and the writer ends up feeling frustrated and unfulfilled. The second type attempts to have the handwriting look perfect—as though a grammar schoolteacher had written it in the perfect cursive style. The third type is concerned with the content of the letter. This type will reread the letter and question whether what is felt is really being expressed; these writers will be concerned about how their child feels about what is written. They might fear sounding too rigid, too emotional, too angry, etc.

If you find yourself in a perfectionist mode, here are two strategies to help you move through it:

a. Imaging and creative visualization are useful techniques for the perfectionist. We suggest you close your eyes and visualize yourself writing. As you begin to write you find yourself not knowing where to go with the topic you have chosen. You are not quite sure what you want to say. As you watch yourself risk forging ahead with writing the letter, you see yourself smiling. You see yourself happy to be able to stay with the writing even though it is uncomfortable. You see yourself crossing out sentences or words here and there. You see yourself content with the fact that you are able to keep going, even though your letter is not perfect. You actually hear yourself say, "It cannot be perfect . . . it's best just as it is."

b. Perfectionists fear failure. Remind yourself that there is no way to fail at this writing process. You are the guide, you are the author, you write the rules. There isn't even a way that you can make mistakes in this process—your thoughts and feelings cannot be wrong, and therefore the letter cannot be a failure. As Karl Menniger said, "Fears are educated into us and can be educated out" (*Touchstones for Men*).

Before ending this section, we feel there is one more topic for discussion—perfectionism and parenting. If you can allow yourself to be imperfect in your writing you will be doing yourself and your child a great favor and service. How can this be so?

If you strive to write perfect letters you might also strive to be a perfect parent. Having a fantasy that the perfect parent exists is setting yourself up for failure.

In the process of writing this book and talking with parents-to-be, we met a young couple, Dave and Marsha. Dave was thirty-five and Marsha was thirty-two. They were married and had a three-year-old son. When they heard about our journal they were both very interested in beginning one of their own. At the time Marsha was four months pregnant with their second child. They started by writing together at night. Each time they started to write Dave became very frustrated; he felt that his real feelings did not come through, that his writing was too messy, or that his child wouldn't like what he wrote. When he and his wife read their letters to each other he always felt inferior because he compared himself to her. He felt his writing just wasn't good enough.

After a month Marsha suggested they meet with us to help him move beyond these feelings of frustration and inadequacy. When we all met Dave had already stopped writing letters and Marsha felt she was left with the responsibility of completing the journal. It became clear to us that this was what always happened between Marsha and Dave. When Dave didn't do something perfectly he withdrew. This had also occurred in the parenting of their three-year-old son; Dave wasn't a good enough dad so he stayed later at the office, worked on weekends, and withdrew from the family. This example shows how perfectionism affects the family and the parenting process.

During our brief meeting the "bell went off" for Dave and Marsha. They both now understood that they had some work to do together. Dave agreed he would not hide at work and that they would continue the journal writing process separately and together.

A beginning step in parenting in general is to realize that it is a process of experimentation. There is no perfect formula. However, there are guidelines available to support parents and parents-to-be. One source we highly recommend is *Your Baby and Child from Birth to Age Five* by Penelope Leach, Ph.D. This book and others offer suggestions, recommendations, or ideas about parenting and coping with difficult situations.

Your perfectionism impacts the entire family. If you strive for perfection you are teaching your child that it is a positive trait to have. On the other hand, you are giving your child a gift if you allow him or her to see your imperfections and to realize that you are not perfect. It's useful for your children to see that you too have to learn and practice something before you master it.

Acknowledgments

We have had a wonderful time writing and designing Letters for Tomorrow: A Journal for Expectant Moms and Dads. There are many people we would like to thank for helping bring this book to life. They are:

- Susan Golomb, our talented literary agent, who believed in this book from its inception. Susan's editorial comments, tender care, perseverance, and insight brought us to Doubleday;

- Lori Lipsky, our editor at Main Street/Doubleday, whose editing, design ideas, and marketing strategies have added greatly to the quality and beauty of our book;

- Lisa Freeman for her magnificent art;

- The wonderful expectant moms and dads who shared their letters with us and allowed us to include them in the book;

- Bob Gibson, who guided us and the book in a very special way; and

- Our families (Nat, Matthew, Michael, Katie, and Johnnie) and friends for their love, kindness, laughter, and support throughout the birth of this book.

We hope in the years to come there will be many moments when you reflect back on your pregnancy, thoroughly delighting in what was written.

Warmly,

Robin and Cathy

Bibliography

Brinkley, Ginny; Goldberg, Linda; Kukar, Janice. *A Guide to Prepared Birth from Pregnancy to Parenthood.* New York: Avery Publishing Group, Inc., 1988.

Eisenberg, Arlene; Murkoff, Heidi E.; Hathway, Sandee E., B.S.N. *What to Expect When You're Expecting.* New York: Workman Publishing, 1984.

Hotchner, Tracie. *Pregnancy and Childbirth—the Complete Guide.* New York: Avon Books, 1984.

Kelly, Kate. *Sesame Street Magazine,* Parents' Guide article. May 1992.

Leach, Penelope. *Your Baby and Child from Birth to Age Five.* New York: Alfred A. Knopf, 1987.

Nilsson, Lennart. *A Child Is Born.* New York: Delacorte Press/Seymour Lawrence, 1990.

Progoff, Ira. *At a Journal Workshop: The Basic Text and Guide for Using the Intensive Journal Process.* New York: Dialogue House Library, 1975.

Rainer, Tristine. *The New Diary.* Los Angeles: Jeremy P. Tarcher, Inc., 1978.

Spock, Benjamin, M.D., and Rothenberg, Michael, M.D. *Dr. Spock's Baby and Child Care.* New York: Pocket Books, 1985.

Stoddard, Alexandra. *Gift of a Letter.* New York: Doubleday, 1990.

About the Authors

Robin Freeman Bernstein is a licensed Marriage, Family, and Child Therapist. She is married and the mother of a six-year-old son, Matthew. Cathy Moore is a licensed Clinical Psychologist. She is also married and the mother of a seventeen-year-old daughter, Katie, and a thirteen-year-old son, Johnnie. Through years of private practice, and in a number of ventures as partners, they have helped guide hundreds of clients—children, adolescents, adults, couples, and families—to better understand themselves and maximize their full potential.

The authors are currently working on a series of letter journals focusing on the different stages of life.

About the Artist

Lisa Freeman is an illustrator and writer. Ms. Freeman lives in Southern California, where she enjoys the ocean and works in her studio. She is a published poet and is currently illustrating a book for the "Safe Moves" program to educate children about traffic and dealing with strangers.